21 Years

21 Years

A Collection of Poems on Leadership

Vincent A. Watson

Charleston, SC
www.PalmettoPublishing.com

21 Years…A Collection of Poems on Leadership

Copyright © 2023 by Vincent A. Watson

All rights reserved

No portion of this book may be reproduced, stored in a retrieval system, or transmitted in any form by any means–electronic, mechanical, photocopy, recording, or other–except for brief quotations in printed reviews, without prior permission of the author.

First Edition

Paperback: 979-8-8229-0380-7
eBook: 979-8-8229-0381-4

This book is dedicated to the challenges of leadership and people who make us better leaders.

Table of Contents

Part I: Leading Yourself 1
   1   Leadership 3
   2   Leadership Vision 6
   3   Accountability 8
   4   Confidence 10
   5   Lead Yourself 12
   6   Self-Aware 14
   7   Humility 16
   8   Courage 18
   9   Critical Thinking 20
  10   Empathy 22
  11   Integrity 24
  12   Open Minded 26
  13   Growth 29
  14   Patience With Yourself 32

Part II: Leading Others 35
  15   Teacher 37
  16   Mentor 39
  17   Leadership Support 42
  18   Communication 44
  19   Listening 46
  20   Fairness 48
  21   Synergy 50
  22   Social Intellect 52
  23   Inspiration 54
  24   Patience with Others 55

Part III: Parting Thoughts 57
    25 Two Types of Leaders. 59
    26 The Toxic Leader. 62
    27 What Happened to Leadership 64

About the Author 67

Part I: Leading Yourself

1
Leadership

There are countless books on what traits a leader needs to find success

This is because most leaders lead from their position and leadership traits they don't possess

The age-old question is a leader made or is a leader born

The nature versus nurturer origin of a leader debate marches on

Personally, I believe it's a combination

I feel leaders are born with a desire to lead and that desire drives them to pursue education

What's the difference between someone who manages and someone who leads

If want to maintain the status quo get a manager, yes indeed

But if you want someone to take your organization to the next level a leader is what you need

A manager maintains the status quo

Their focus is consistency not to make the business grow

A leader creates a vision

When choosing a leader, the ability to see the big picture should be part of the decision

A leader has the courage to make tough decisions and to let people make mistakes

This is difficult for most people because their reputation and evaluation are at stake

21 Years...

A leader is selfless and cares about his people more than his career
The last statement is powerful, because people make the leader, and this isn't always clear
A leader values communication
Understands that the success of the organization
Is founded in the exchange of information
A leader is patient and takes time and care in implementing their plan
Change is slow a process and takes time is something they understand
Vision and Patience are nothing without the other they go hand in hand
A leader is open minded and allows creativity to flow
They accept they have blind spots and things they don't know
A leader is fair and holds everyone to the same expectation
This is not only true in their words, but also in their demonstration
A leader is an integrator and creates collective energy
We discuss this in greater detail in the poem titled "Synergy"
By default, a leader is a mentor
Determined and equipped to take their employees to levels never experienced before
A leader also thinks critically
They can find solutions and solve problems regardless of how challenging the issue might be
The best leaders are usually self-aware
They understand who they desire to be, and they must overcome biases because they are there
A leader utilizes social intellect

They understand that emotions and perspectives create a deeper connect
A leader places a strong emphasis on their ability to listen
They understand employees make the leader - not the position
Leaders develop their leadership skill by leading themselves first from within - internally
They apply these lessons learned to be more effective with others externally
A leader is a constant source of inspiration
They know how to change the climate to get most out of their people in any situation
A leader is a person of integrity
In all situations and with all people they deal honestly
A leader is humble and meek
They don't flaunt their status this makes them strong instead of weak
A leader owns their actions takes complete accountability
Of what happens and fails to happen as their responsibility
All these traits a leader must possess
If they desire to find any level of leadership success

2

Leadership Vision

As a leader you get paid to see
The future and how to create a greater reality
The vision is yours, but the implementation is a shared responsibility
A vision is a picture of the future that's not so far away
It consists of goals and includes a mission statement to guide you day to day
Without a vision it's impossible to implement change there's no other way
But be cautious because communicating the need for change can be tough to convey
To start your vision ask yourself how do you define success?
Is it profits, being more efficient, and/or happy personnel, you want to address?
A leader must have a vision for where they're leading an organization too
This is one of the most important things a leader is required to do
A leader is one person, but requires the skills of a few
As a leader must understand the organization and the people too
Excellent managerial skills, this is nothing new
Many leaders have failed because when it came to managing they couldn't buy a clue

Understanding the organization provides insight into
The challenges you may face when leading the organization through
Change based on the vision created by you
Understanding the people will help you see things from their view
This will create buy-in and convince people to support you
Study and understand the organization and people
before you make a move
Without understanding the transition will be far from smooth
When creating a vision don't go in blind
The absolute best starting point is with the end in mind
Look into the future and then rewind
A vision that's perfectly aligned
Is one that's designed
To contain the current status and future goals combined

3

Accountability

No one man has ever achieved organizational goals alone
So, it's important that leaders account for everything that happens as their own
This means everything the team does and fails to do
Is a direct reflection of your leadership and falls on you
As a leader most responsibilities you will delegate
The key is learning to stay involved and knowing when you should participate
As a leader you must master the hands-off approach
Your position will require you to stand along the sideline and coach
Nothing can change the fact that as the leader you are the boss
You will be praised for achievements and questioned when there's a loss
As a leader you will account for the direction of the organization by creating a vision
You will guide the business along this path with critical thinking and the final decision
As a leader you're most accountable for having the right information
This starts with age old art of communication
As a leader you don't need to know everything - stay out of the weeds
Master your craft and understand exactly what information you need

To ensure the organization is moving forward and following your lead

Create an expectation of communication requirements and information flow

Focus on the things at your level - trust subordinate leaders to Handle everything below

Don't be guilty of being a bad manager a "micro"

Spend your time understanding vital information and how it's developed and processed

Discuss with managers to determine if there are ways to eliminate waste or excess

Finding more efficient ways to do things is what an accountable leader would address

Accountability in leadership requires a lot of trust

It's impossible to be in all places at all times - so trust is an absolute must

As I stated leadership and accountability is an art

To be at more than one place at the same time understanding is what you must impart

As a leader you must inform and educate your managers on what's most important to you

This can be in the form of dollars, hours, or manpower just to name a few

Focus on the quality of information - the what - not necessarily the how to

Once management understand what's most important to you

Magically you have now multiplied yourself times two

Remember your accountable for all your organization does and fails to do

4

Confidence

We're all confident to a certain degree
The things we're not confident in - is because of a level of uncertainty
What's certain for you is not necessarily certain for me
So, we're not confident in all things because of the difference in our talent and ability
So, what is confidence
It's a combination of experience and competence
Confidence increases with time - without it we can only remain ignorant
Confidence is believing in your God given talents
Arrogance is loud but confidence is silent
Confidence is understanding and accepting who you are
This is the most important type of confidence by far
Acceptance means you're thankful for being alive
Always appreciate the gift and seek to grow and thrive
Confidence is trusting in your skills
If you don't have confidence in yourself no one else will
Confidence can be felt in all you say and do
Confidence is contagious, so others catch it too

With confidence sometimes you expect to fail
Knowing that failure teaches you a lesson and that you will overcome and prevail
When you're confident you always give your best
Even when trials come to put your confidence to the test
Confidence is trusting in what you believe
Apply effort to confidence and there's no limit to what you can achieve
Confidence is knowing the "why" behind your values and what you stand for
Confidence is all things and so much more
Confidence doesn't come free but it's something we can all earn
The most confident leaders are usually very confident in their ability to learn
So, if you're not confident in your ability to lead
Time and experience will develop the confidence you need
If I could remove the word confidence from the dictionary
"Love Yourself" would replace it in everyone's vocabulary

5
Lead Yourself

Leadership lessons begin
When you first learn to lead yourself from within
Why is this true?
Because people will judge your words, but judge your actions times two
If don't lead yourself well!
You can't run from the lack of self-leadership others can tell
So, if you desire to succeed
Let yourself be the first person you lead
Personal leadership starts with a personal vision for yourself
Like, obtaining more education or improving your health
Similar to an organizational vision like generating more wealth
Leading yourself teaches you the power of discipline
To achieve your goals through consistent action over and over again
There will be moments when your goals and thoughts don't align
Remain focused, disciplined, and you will be just fine
Once you overcome and put challenges behind you
You will have a greater appreciation for the challenges of others too
These things you might not have considered or understood before
Being a leader goes beyond position it requires much more

Achieving personal goals teaches a lesson that's not so clear to see
This lesson is in Accountability
Taking account for every choice you make
Understanding how your actions impact your goal and what's at stake
Leaders are accountable for achieving the vision of the organization
You will decide how to achieve the goal, but this requires others and their participation
learning to account for yourself provides you with this experience and education
When leading yourself you discover that change is a slow process
Change requires patience and in time you will make progress
Patience is something all leaders must embrace
When you practice patience with yourself, you extend to others the same measure of grace
Leading yourself teaches you to communicate
To inspire yourself into action and to motivate
In moments of weakness and times when you don't feel so great
When your team lacks motivation, you're able to relate
You're also able to connect
This is better known as emotional intellect
Leading yourself provides you with invaluable experience and insight
Overall, leadership is a matter of all your mind not all your might

6
Self-Aware

Self-awareness is the process of looking at yourself from a dual perspective
It consists of input of others, but mostly introspective
Understanding who you are and who you desire to be is the main objective
It's the process of establishing standards and to those standards you compare
Your thoughts, actions, and emotions until you grow there
If the concept of self-awareness is new
It's seeking change by understanding why you do what you do
Along with how your thoughts influence your actions and your actions impact others too
This is a personal affair
You may not understand you're bias, although not seen they're in there
If you're biased, how can you possibly be fair?
Not only to your team but to yourself - this is the road to nowhere
Self-Awareness is a constant evaluation
Of your thoughts - actions and then seeking to understand this information
To improve yourself - which will in turn improve the organization
When situations arise and you don't perform to the standard you set

Replay the event in your mind and make sure you obtain all the understanding you can get
Once your thoughts and actions are understood
Rate yourself - was your performance bad - neutral - or was it good
You can also rate your performance on a scale from one to ten
Regardless be honest in your assessment - this is where improvement begin
When you desire to change you must evaluate your thoughts and actions over and over again
The assessment is truly a gift to treasure
Keep in mind that you can't change what you don't measure
Don't let a less than desired assessment get you down
Keep your head up and strive to score higher the next time around
If improvement through Self-Awareness is what you desire to achieve
To change our actions, we must first change what we believe
Self-Awareness may uncover some ugly truths about yourself
Accept these truths - but determine if this belief still serves you - this is good for your mental health
The roots of some of your truths may be buried deep in your mind
To understand these beliefs, you must relive and do a rewind
Travel the history of this belief until you discover
When you gave birth to this belief and only then can you uncover
How this belief influences your actions
In this moment you can abort what you believe and do a new thing according to your satisfaction

7
Humility

Humility is the ability to not think of yourself as more than you should be
Because truthfully you may consider yourself a great leader, but you won't be everyone's cup of tea
It's about stepping down off your pedestal
And being found to be upright instead of a downright fool
Some leaders fail because they become too arrogant or too great
Humility is about maintaining your status, but being able to relate
To everyone - This is what makes humility such a valuable trait
Humility opens our hearts and mind to listen
So, humble yourself and understand respect is earned through action not position
A humble leader operates with a servant's heart and an agile mind
Your actions aren't self-serving, they're more about serving mankind
So, splash yourself with a dose humility each and every day
Because the price of arrogance is too big of a price to pay
You ever heard the phrase the more people that work for you the more people you work for?
Read this over again if you haven't heard this before

When operating with humility you acknowledge your ignorance and things you don't know
Humility allows you accept your blind spots so you're able to learn and grow
With humility you understand there's always more to learn
Suggestion - spend your time learning about people and their trust you will earn
Attention and understanding are what people yearn
Yes, you're the leader and this is true
But with humility you accept that your subordinates are more knowledgeable than you
Knowing more about their job is what you should expect them to do
This frees you from having to do their job and yours too
As a leader there will be many problems you must solve
Humbly listen to others - because finding solutions is easier with the more people you involve
With humility you understand your tenure will come end
The organization was there before you and will be there after, this is reality my friend
Can I recommend
That you mentor and train others and your influence will extend
If we build leaders, we will impact the world time and time again

8

Courage

Courage can't be taught in school or learned in a seminar
Courage is a trait you're born with it's part of who you are
So, are leaders born or made is still up for debate
I still say both, but qualities like courage is something you can't formally educate
We must analyze each trait
And ask if it's a quality or skill
Qualities are things no man can take away or instill
You're born with it, but unlike a quality, you can develop a skill with desire and will
I know some may say a courageous leader that's not me
But trust we all have it, to some level and degree
You may show little courage, while others show it more frequently
Regardless of how much you show and what you level may be
I know for a fact and without a doubt
At some point a leadership challenge will force you to bring it out
This is what becoming a courageous leader is all about
Courage is truly a foundational trait
Meaning that it's the difference between the good and the great
There are many colors to courage, but it's something all leaders require
The courage to charge a hill or run into a burning building is a courage most admire

But I'm not talking about the type of courage in which you to expose yourself to fire
I'm talking about the most basic level of courage that will be required of you
The ability to make a decision and to see it through
Leaders are expected to make tough decisions; this is nothing new
You will have to decide the what, when, where, and the how to,
Who to promote and who not to, just to name a few
At first you may overthink your decisions and even second guess
First be sure you're being fair and second, you're doing what's best
However, a taste of fear may set in
This is where the need to have courage truly begin
As time goes on you will move beyond fear and fear less
Understand that your courage will face a series of challenges and tests
Before you become a leader who's worthy to be called courageous

2
Critical Thinking

Critical thinking is like hindsight being foresight and understanding what happens next
Why is it called critical thinking - let me put this into context
To think critically there are a few things you must know like the back of your hand
These things include the organizational goals and the organizational plan
Your vision, goals, and everyone above you and those under the voice of your command
Critical thinking is understanding the big picture and how everything and everyone interact
You can quickly identify the disconnects and impact
To make decisions that move the organization forward while keeping everything intact
Critical thinking is the ability to quickly make the best decision for all involved to be exact
When thinking critically you can't let your emotions distract
If you become too emotional you may overreact
Feel your emotions and let them flow through you, but always stick to the facts

In critical thinking you recognize when problems arise in which you shape and define
You understand how and where problem(s) and organizational goals don't align
You listen attentively to different perspectives, recommendations, and suggestions
Then turn around and ask the right questions
Critical thinking involves keen observation
And the ability to quickly digest and process all information
While considering all parties involved and stages of execution
You develop feasible and valid solutions
Most assume critically thinking requires you to be on a higher level mentally
This true to some degree
Overall, thinking critically
Is a combination of these three.
Insight, Understanding, and History
This was never explained to me
As a leader you will fail to make the right decision - it's not a crime
Trust me the ability to solve problems and think critically develops with time

10

Empathy

Oftentimes leaders use their position to hide and conceal
Their emotions and how they really feel
Not willing to step from the behind the mask of leadership and reveal
That they're human and their heart beats are real
It seems as if being a human with emotions is less than ideal
Which leaves no room for empathy
Compassion or even sympathy
So, everyone is a position or nothing more than an employee
Not someone's father, mother, brother, sister or someone with a family
When you're able to empathize
You unmask yourself and realize
A leader is just a human being in disguise
When you remove the mask - you're able to relate and to connect
In the only way which matters to all - life and the human aspect
When you've found the freedom as a leader to be a Human Being
Your eyes awaken and see what your employees are seeing
You understand that everyone is doing the best they can
An empathic leader can connect to both the professional as well as the man

Some situations will require an emotional intervention
As a leader you'll need the ability to transition
From professional into the Human Dimension
Life doesn't always play out as we hope or expect
Some employees will try to play on your emotions and even disrespect
Empathy reminds us that no one person is perfect
Emotions are in all we say and do - so empathy is the foundation for Emotional Intellect

11

Integrity

As a leader your integrity will be tested by the flame
Many leaders have been burned for the lack of integrity that it's impossible to name
Once their career thrived, but ended in shame
Their fall from grace is now their claim to fame
These leaders operated with integrity of the lowest degree
It wasn't about what's best for the team, it was more about what's best for me
When it comes to integrity you deal honestly
With yourself first and others secondly
You do the hard right regardless how easy the wrong might be
Guided by strong ethics you do what's right
While in plain view of others and when you're out of sight
Because what's done in the dark will eventually come to light
To lead with integrity, you must put your pride aside
Own your mistakes and don't try to hide
This can only happen if you hold strong ethical principles inside
A leader of integrity is worthy of trust
Not easily swayed or convinced to give into their lust
As a person of influence, power, and control this is a must

It will be very tempting to sell your soul
To tell half-truths, but a full lie as a whole
And believe you can get away with it because of your position and role
A person of integrity is humble - not concerned with power or greed
They focus on the bigger picture and taking care of everyone they lead
They deal honestly in word and in deed
They give to others even if it means sacrificing what they need
Don't get caught up in pursuing status or reputation
That your dishonest dealings make headlines across the nation
Set the example and expectation
That you're a leader of integrity and expect it of everyone as your declaration

12

Open Minded

Just like most things that work best when open so does your mind
After years of experience sometimes we forget we have spots called blind
And maybe, just maybe our methods and techniques are antiquated and years behind
We believe this way will work, and this won't
Our personal list of the dos and don'ts
We have certain methods we like to prescribe or to propose
Not realizing that this is a sign that our minds are closed
Maybe this is true for all leaders I suppose
But I challenge you to be more reflective
And to try and see things from a different perspective
Allow people to be creative, and don't be so directive
Letting people do what's comfortable for them is very effective
We all have experiences and insights this is true
But have you considered another point of view?
What about putting on and taking a walk in another man's shoe?
To think we know and have experienced it all is so easy to do
Keep in mind - that what works well for you may not work for others too

This is true today and will remain true for every year beyond two thousand and twenty-two
Open your mind because you may actually learn something new
What's most important to you?
To tell people the what and the how to
Or that the job gets done
With the advancement of technology there are many ways to do things a lot more than one
Simply listening to the ideas and thoughts of others is nothing more than information
When you open your mind to receive ideas you inspire communication
You create excitement and this will increase participation
When the team accepts and respects the perspectives of each other is a powerful combination
This is the formula for a connected and productive organization
When you acknowledge the ideas of others and give them a voice
It's takes nothing from you as a leader the final decision is still your choice
Some ideas will gain your approval and others you will reject
Regardless, always display openness, acceptance, and most important respect
This is important because everyone is watching and your actions they will reflect

21 Years...

Unfortunately, this is where some leaders fall
Because they think as the leader that must be all knowing and know it all
Remember the power to make the decision belongs to you it's your call
Open your mind allow others to express ideas is healthy and wise
But you must ensure every voice is respected no compromise
If not, this will lead to the team's demise
The concept of an open mind is to remove blind spots and things we may not see
It also creates the collective energy we talk about in "Synergy"
When you let go and open your mind to receive
There's no level the team can't reach or achieve

13

Growth

Ask a person how to grow
And you'll be surprised at how many do not know
Most people think growth just happens - it's a natural process
If this was true there wouldn't be as many bad leaders, there would be a lot less
My belief is age comes naturally and you must be intentional about making progress
Truth is - the leader you were when you first entered through the door
Isn't enough because times are ever changing, and the position will require more
So how do you grow to be better than before?
May I recommend finding a good book and a good mentor
A good book is full of experiences, thoughts, opinions, and they vary far and wide
A different perspective is what a good book can provide
Receive the information - but understand growth happens when it's applied
This will require self-awareness for you to look inside
To get out, test your understanding, and to make mistakes
Learning from your failures equals growth this is what it takes
Mentors are great because they've walked in your shoes and understand what the job require
It's best to follow someone whose journeyed further than you especially if you hope to go higher

21 Years...

For mentors time is money and for some their time is quite expensive
Take complete advantage of your time with them - and Thankful for the time they give
A mentor can provide insight, knowledge, and then some
The biggest benefit of a mentor is their wisdom
So, give mentors an open ear
To help you grow personally and in your career
Or you may want to consider a more costly approach
And hire an Executive Coach
These professionals will analyze your behavior from top to bottom and each and every action
Their job is to understand your strengths and weaknesses and how to maximize your interactions
So, they will review everything from job performance to customer satisfaction
A good Executive Coach is money well spent
After all investing in yourself is one of the greatest investments
Or you can take the path that will cost you nothing, it's absolutely free
Asking for feedback from an employee
In this approach you can't be a person that's easy to offend
You must be able to receive constructive feedback without trying to defend
Remember you asked them to be a critic not your friend
I also recommend that you follow-up and ask employees if you've made progress every now and then

Regardless of how many or what approach you pursue
Put time and energy into your growth and becoming
a better you

14

Patience With Yourself

A leader is someone you grow into
Be patient in your growth and development and you'll become a leader too
When we first enter any level of leadership it's all positional
Our influence is based on our position, it's one dimensional
The transition into leadership requires time it's truly transitional
Yes, you were selected based on your achievements,
but also your potential
A leader must lead themselves and learn to lead others they are influential
It takes time to learn how to effectively communicate
To inspire others to be great
To learn how to synergize a team and to integrate
Being able to do this on day one sounds great
But chances are you're going to have a lot on your plate
So much that you may not be able to see clearly or think straight
This is how the development process flows
Like the saying you'll be drinking from a fire hose
Everything will be coming at you at a rapid pace
It will feel like you're trying to pack too much into your head space

In time things will begin to slow down
You're able to keep your head above water and no longer feel like you're about to drown
You've learned the people, the system, and the process
You're now moving away from stress and toward success
Now it feels like the world revolves in the palm of your hand
People not only respect the position, but they also respect the man
This officially marks your transition
From being a leader solely based on position
One day you'll look back and wonder where the time went
You'll find yourself telling others to take their time and to be patient in their development

Part II: Leading Others

15
Teacher

The workplace is like a classroom - where learning is an ongoing process
We are all ignorant on something - "all knowing" is a title no man can possess
There's always more to learn
This is true for everyone regardless of position or how much you earn
Mistakes always equate to a loss
In both time and money - Teaching others can help avoid these costs
When leaders become teachers, problems slowly fade away
That's one less costly mistake you must pay
All leaders strive to be great
But the greatest of them all are those who teach and educate
Because teaching helps not only to integrate but accelerate
Performance to a large degree although on the job is school from which you never graduate
Teaching will extend your influence and control
If you're a successful teacher, you'll find yourself on a list called the Honor Roll
As a leader class is always in session
Teachers are always prepared to offer wisdom through a well-timed lesson
Whether the lesson is on life or on the profession

21 Years...

Teaching others is time well spent
This is true for when speaking to a group or an individual assignment
Growth minded leaders create a learning environment
You can drop knowledge on employees in the hallway as they pass
The workplace is a learning environment where there is always an opportunity for class
Meetings are the perfect time to expand and teach on topic being addressed
Sharing your insights and stories of your experience sets everyone up for success
Your stories may come from a time in the past
Teaching builds trust and if you're a good teacher you'll build it fast
Teaching is an art, so you need to mix up your approach
Some moments will require you to be direct - at other times you need to coach
Understand you are working with professionals so always show respect
For their experience and their intellect
Some teaching moments may only consist of a simple suggestion
Practice the science of self-discovery by asking them lead-in questions
In this way you given them the assignment and space to best receive the lesson
You also facilitate growth and inspire the desire to learn
Employees who experience leaders that teach become teachers in-turn

16

Mentor

The job of a mentor is to provide understanding and to challenge perspective
To help mentees choose the right tools to ensure they're effective
That they're equipped to handle a variety of situations is the main objective
Mentees have little experience, so their tool bag consist of a small selection
Mentors both sharpens tools and introduce new ones to add to the mentees collection
Mentorship works because mentees are on a road headed in the mentor's direction
The very road the mentor once traveled so there's a level of familiarity and a connection
Mentorship is like knowing now what you wish you knew then
The mistakes you made during your journey, your mentee won't repeat again
Mentorship provides you with the opportunity to tell your story
Each one is unique and connected to a tool in your inventory
So, drill down deep inside
To access all the tools, you've obtained as a result of your failures and the things you've tried
As a mentor you are the ultimate tool guide

21 Years...

Mentorship requires a serious commitment and participation
It takes time to teach the concept of each tool and its application
Mentorship is real world education
Patience is needed to explain the in's and out of each tool
These things can't be learned in school
Bottom line a mentors reach
Goes far beyond those who only teach
Mentorship will require you to expose some of your personal thoughts and views
Be wise in what you share and understand what information they can and cannot use
In the end mentorship will create memories you both will treasure
The lasting impact of mentorship is something no tape can measure
Leaders do your part to ensure the wheel of mentorship continues to spin around and around
Because mentees become mentors and continue to pass the lessons down
But be cautious don't try to mentor everyone
Leave that decision to the mentee
Because you won't connect with everyone and you're not everyone's cup of tea
Mentorship doesn't cost anything, but is your time truly free?
Take this from me
You don't want the stress
Of pouring your heart and soul into someone who's not striving for success

This wisdom is time tested
You can't help anyone if they're not invested
So, make sure they're all in first
If not, instead of moving forward you'll find yourself moving in reverse
Keep in mind time is something, no man gets back, and something no man can reimburse

17

Leadership Support

Leaders support their employee's growth and development
But you must understand the goals of the employee to ensure the support is relevant
This shows that developing others is your top priority
Which helps to increase your leadership authority
When you make developing others a main concern
You not only build future leaders - but you'll get respect in return
As a leader you support your employee's professional goals and dreams
Also, their personal interests regardless of how unusual they seem
The goal of every leader should be to uplift and support their entire team
Support is maintaining an open line of communication
Giving employees direction through the dissemination of information
Support is shielding your employees from being attacked
It's important that your employees understand that you have their back
Support is also making yourself available as a resource
Your mentorship and their growth multiply the force
Support is providing them with a listening ear
Remain open minded, patient, and understanding with what you hear

In support you empower their decision
This is easy if it's aligned with your vision
You provide support by addressing concerns
The more concerns you address the more trust you'll earn
You will also support their family and their needs
Indirectly they're a part of your team because they're also impacted by your ability to lead
Support can be summed up in one statement I guess
As a leader you support your employees and their success

18

Communication

The ability to communicate goes far beyond what's said
Effective communication clearly paints a picture of what's in our head
This is true when words are spoken and when they're read
The best communicators don't speak their language they speak the language of others instead
These communicators clearly translate
Thoughts and ideas into words, so they create
Verbal translations that facilitate
Understanding - so the receiver can relate
The quality of your communication will dictate
If you're a good leader or a great
So, it would be wise to invest in learning to effectively communicate
Overall, communication is the exchange of information
Most don't fail with the content they fail in the application
Always consider the audience before your presentation
You'll responsible for what you say, but not what's heard
So it's important to think before you speak a single word
Take a moment to put yourself in their shoes
Imagine how they will respond once you present the news
Again, be selective with the words you choose
The purpose of communication is to connect
Emotions need to be considered; I suggest reading the poem on "Social Intellect"

A successful connection is a powerful force
Imagine plugging into a power source
One of unlimited potential and supply
Connecting is understanding the information and the why
Failing to address the why is where some connections die
Communication is directly related to your ability to influence and control
If you effectively communicate with individuals, you'll influence the team as whole
Learning to communicate effectively will be an ongoing process
Take the time to read people and you will be sure to achieve success

19

Listening

The ability to listen is a skill
Listening is hearing what's said along with the emotion they feel
Listening is a form of validation if you will
Regardless of what's said and heard
Your only job as a listener is to receive every word
To be sure an exchange has occurred
Practice an active ear,
Rephrase based on your understanding and then ask questions to be clear
This will remove any doubt and fear
And expose what you misunderstood and failed to hear
This creates a win-win
To start the process of listening, we must learn to suspend
And not hang-on or spend
Time on our thoughts, judgements, and listening to the voice within
Learning to listen is not a matter of if, but a matter of when
Know that your ability to listen will be tested time and time again
Leaders please ensure - that if your listening skills was given a score
It would be favorable - passing, and not rated as poor
So, when you engage in conversation you leave with more understanding than before

If this is the opposite of what you do
Then the only person you can hear is "You"
Please look in the mirror and remind yourself that
a conversation takes "Two"
Sometimes we pretend to listen only to have our say
This is still a form of you listening to yourself on display
As a leader this is a game you don't want to play
Strive to be a rich listener because understanding and
knowledge creates wealth
Make it a habit to listen to others outside of yourself
Learning to listen is an area in which we all can grow
Why have a conversation only to confirm what you already
think you know?
So, give people the freedom to speak and make them feel heard
If you want to build trust as a leader, knowing how to listen
is the most preferred
Please understand me
That when you let people talk it doesn't mean that you agree
You can totally disagree
Listening only means that they are free
To express themselves, regardless of what the situation
might be
Unfortunately, sometimes leaders don't seek to understand
The situation at hand
They only seek to address the employee and fail to address
the man
Always seek to get to the heart of the matter if you can
Listening costs, you nothing and comes in unlimited supply
Never forget that that listening will get you things that money
can't buy

20

Fairness

What does it mean to be fair?
Simple
To treat everyone equally with understanding and care
To praise and punish to the same degree and same effect
To treat everyone with dignity and respect
When being fair you don't select
Who you will and will not support or protect?
This is the opposite of fair, this is neglect
Being fair is learning not to place anyone on a pedestal
Self-Awareness and understanding your biases are great tools
Fairness is giving everyone the same opportunity to succeed
It's all about putting them in the best position and knowing how to feed
Them with the information and opportunities they need
To go above and beyond and to exceed
As the leader everyone will follow your lead
So always be fair in word and in deed
Sometimes being fair will take all that you got
Truthfully, some you feel will deserve it, others you may not
So where do you start?
A formal explanation of expectations would be smart
From these expectations you should never depart
Because this could tear your reputation apart

And life could quickly turn into a nightmare
Because now you're on the fast track to being considered a leader who's unfair
You must display fairness in all you say and do
Whether you know it or not someone is always watching you
So be ever present and aware
And always behave as if someone else was listening or standing right there
And when talking with someone never ever compare
Them to anyone this situation could prove to be difficult to repair
And this could negatively impact both you and the work atmosphere
No leader can afford to put this bad vibe in the air
Please don't play "favorites" you don't ever want to go there
Being fair, like most things is easier said than done
Because you won't feel the same way about everyone
Great leaders treat and make all feel as if they are somebody and someone

21

Synergy

Is the collective energy
Of everyone working toward the goal
Operating as individuals and as part of the whole
Some leaders never realize
That their ability to succeed is tied to their ability to synergize
Synergizing will require you to integrate
Different frames of thoughts and walks of life to facilitate
The team's ability to coexist and effectively communicate
Along with an environment in which everyone wants to participate
Understanding everyone's strengths and weaknesses is key
To know where to position and to use them effectively
Nothing kills a team faster than someone not knowing where they fit in
If anyone feels left out or disrespected, it's impossible for the team to win
Synergizing will require you to make everyone feel like a part of the team time and time again
Remember a team is only as strong as the weakest link
As a leader it's your job to ensure the team is connected and everyone is in sync
Synergy is a balancing act
Probably one of the most challenging as a matter of fact

It not only requires understanding, but it also requires tact
So, if you want to synergize and keep your team intact
Be proactive in understanding your team and how they interact
Teams fall apart when leaders are forced to react
Fail to create synergy and you will create division
A path toward an eventual collision
A team traveling the wrong direction and crashing into your vision
So, it should come as no surprise
The failure to synergize
Will only lead to a team's demise
So, it would be wise
That you understand each member and see things from their eyes
This is true for all teams regardless of size
Understand that conflicts will arise
Remain positive and recognize
That this is only an opportunity for you to exercise
Your ability to visualize and strategize
In order to synergize
All teams experience a series of lows before they experience a series of highs
When you create synergy positive energy will overflow
When this happens there's no limit to what the team can achieve or how high they can go

22

Social Intellect

Social Intellect is what lies under effective communication
It's more than just an exchange of information
Social intelligence is knowing how to interact in any situation
It's understanding your emotions but keeping them under control
This is true if you're interacting with an individual or the team as a whole
Social intellect is understanding that others have emotions too
And that emotion is involved in all we say and do
It's the ability to read these emotions through either a verbal and/or nonverbal clue
It's listening to but quieting the voice in your head
Focusing on people and showing them that you're interested
Social intellect is not about being a social butterfly
It's knowing yourself, how to respond, and understanding why
It's understanding when to speak and when to remain quiet
Sometimes silence speaks louder than words if you haven't tried this you should try it
As a leader many situations and events will challenge your social intellect
Regardless of the situation or event be sure to communicate respect
Things may not always go as you expect
At the end of the day your reputation and image are what you want to protect

You will interact with people more powerful and influential than you
Employees and their families too
There will be events involving the community
Maintaining a personal but business mindset in these situations is key
You may find yourself interacting with grade school kids or those pursuing a higher education
This population usually asks a lot of questions so be prepared to share lots of information
Social intellect will require you to constantly go back to school
To understand events, the people involved, and the social rule
I would advise not to do anything outside of the social norm
At the same time be yourself don't put on a show or perform
Social intelligence is understanding the environment and how to act
This requires self-control and whole lot of tact
If you haven't heard this quote - I've found it to be true
"When in Rome do what the Romans do"

23

Inspiration

A leader must be able to inspire
To push a button that ignites a fire
To motivate the team to reach higher
Inspiration will require
That you understand each person, their dreams, goals, and desire
This is especially important when things come down to the wire
Also, when your team begin to burnout and tire
A leader must be able to reach into the depths of their soul
To find a new level of influence and control
To inspire others into action to reach a goal
You must be able to inspire each individual and the team as a whole
Your ability to inspire your team to achieve
Is directly related to how much they believe
In you as a leader and what they perceive
So, roll up your sleeve
You're the face of the organization
Be inspirational with your words and in your demonstration
Being an example is a very powerful form of inspiration
This form is effective regardless of the generation
Whether you're leading industrialist or those born in the age of information
So, receive this revelation
Inspiration is all in the application

24

Patience with Others

When you look at your employees what do you see?
Do you see them as who they are, or do you see who you need them to be?
When you think of them, do you think of them as people or an employee?
Does your expectation of them match up with reality?
Is this expectation based on performance or their personality?
We need to change our mentality
When it comes to patience with others it's not the who they are but where they are that's key
Let me put it this way
It's about understanding who they may
Grow to be tomorrow, but understanding where they are today
This is where leadership patience comes into play
Leadership is like gardening in which planting seeds is the application
Then we water employees with on the job training and education
And watch them grow as they increase in understanding, knowledge, and information
Sometimes you may feel unsure
If what you planted will grow and mature

21 Years...

Don't react too quickly or premature
Leadership requires patience and the development process is something we must endure
We should look at employees like fertile ground
Meaning that they will soak up and take in everything we give and put down
We should look at them as the highest quality seed
If we're good leaders - gardeners, we will give them all that they need
To sprout to rise above and to succeed
At the same time, we need the courage to uproot
an employee if we sprout a weed
Some soil is more fertile and receptive
Regardless, if you remain patient, you will place things in the proper prospective
Always remain focused on your objective
The goal should be to grow the field - strength is found in numbers the collective
Be patient with everyone don't be selective
This will maximize your ability to be the most effective
Constantly think of ways and opportunities to tend to your field
And in due time positive results you'll yield

Part III: Parting Thoughts

25

Two Types of Leaders

There are only two types of leaders, those who lead out of love and those that lead out of fear
Trust me the difference between these two is evident and very clear
For starters, when you lead out of love, you're Intune with your emotions and the matters of the heart
Those who lead out of fear are more logical and lead with the mind, and believe they're smart
With love you care about others more than your career
Sounds a little counterproductive, but the work of others is what really got you here
The fearful leader only cares about themselves and that's why they lead from fear
With love you understand the more people that work for you the more people you work for
With fear it's their way or no way and they're quick to push you out the door
With love everyone has a voice, and their opinions and thoughts are welcomed and heard
With fear the environment is very tense, intimidating, and people are scared to say a word
With love the leader gives you freedom to make mistakes
Love understands that this is part of the learning process and there's a lesson in every mistake

21 Years...

With fear they micro-manage and they refuse to accept failure no matter what it takes
Remember they live in fear, so they feel their career is always at stake
With love you're given the opportunity to learn, flourish, and grow at your pace
With fear you need to know the job now if not you will be replaced
With love the leader creates a healthy work environment
With fear it's all about stats, metrics, and how much they will earn in retirement
With love the leader ask about your goals, dreams, and what you hope to achieve
With love the leader will support all that you believe
With fear a leader never questions or ask about your goals
Having all the knowledge gives them a sense of power and a sense of control
A leader out of love will share their stories and the lessons they've learned over the years
Most times these stories aren't something you ask for it's something they volunteer
With fear there are no stories to share or to be told
To them knowledge is power and who holds the knowledge holds the gold
With love a leader will provide you mentorship
To make sure you're on path to achieve your dreams and that you're well equipped
With the fearful leader it's all about me
With fear getting to the top is all they see

With fear the leader is all about self
They could care less about your peace of mind or your mental health
As a leader you can only lead like one of the two leaders above
Don't lead with fear, instead I hope you lead with love

26

The Toxic Leader

Have you ever met a toxic leader? Unfortunately, I've met a few
Their motto is do as I say not as I do
They're closed minded to the perspectives of others and refuse to listen
Have you ever met a toxic leader? I have and they only lead by position

Have you ever met a toxic leader? Unfortunately, I've smelt the scent of their perfume
The aroma of their arrogance seems to fill the room
The toxic mix of fear and insecurity makes them explosive like kaboom
Have you ever met a toxic leader? I have and their mission is to devour and consume.

Have you ever met a toxic leader? Unfortunately, I have, and their actions communicate they don't care
They always seem confused, unbalanced, and unaware
Although, physically in your presence - mentally they're off in another world somewhere
Have you ever met a toxic leader? I have and these leaders don't play fair

Have you ever met a toxic leader? Unfortunately, I have, and they demand respect
They show little confidence and even less intellect
Any idea outside of their own they will cast down and reject
Have you ever met a toxic leader? I have met plenty no disrespect

27
What Happened to Leadership

What happened to leadership is no simple explanation
There's a lot of thoughts we need to take into consideration
In my opinion it's not just one thing it's a combination
Like the change in our morals and values as a nation,
And the input that goes into a leader's performance evaluation
Once upon a time, leaders believed in a purpose greater than personal wealth
They supported the organization and put most things before self
They stood for integrity and the greatest value was family and unity
These leaders were also impactful in the community
Leaders of today are only concerned with obtaining the highest leadership position
To glorify themselves and to make the most they can in retirement is their only mission
Leadership is in bad shape "Yes indeed"
So why are some many bad leaders in leadership positions if they can't lead
This may sound strange
But people promote people they like and similar to them and this needs to change
Most of them are excellent managers and that's all good
But the role of a leader is what's misunderstood

Most of them can lead themselves well and meet milestones and that's great
But oftentimes they are so connected to outcomes to others they're unable to relate
They're only concerned with results based on a defined metric
A good leader understands people, the vision, and the business that's the hat trick
These leaders can only lead from position
They understand metrics but fail to understand the human definition
And the people above them are the only people to whom they will listen
When metrics are the only thing a leader can understand and see
There's a high probability
That they lack confidence, fairness, and empathy
They see everyone as a dollar value or just another employee
The job of a leader is tough
When will we wake up and realize the ability to lead yourself is far from enough
Just another consideration
What about changing a leaders performance evaluation
Again, this is usually based on a system of outcomes
That fails to account for their impact on their employees and then some
In addition, the only input usually come from the superiors up above
How about showing the employees and those they lead some love

21 Years...

Meaning let the employees provide input into a leader's performance to a certain percent
If leaders lead people how are outcomes the only performance measurement?
If this happens at some point, maybe we'll question where all the bad leaders went
Unfortunately, if a leader exceeds an outcome, they can find success and succeed
But if you look beyond the outcomes, you will realize these people are unfit to lead
To me it's just seems right
That employees provide feedback on the leader's performance - this will provide valuable insight
And assist in bringing an end to this leadership plight
Leaders of today are more concerned with outcomes than people
This exchange isn't fair and unequal
Instead of change and improvement new leaders are nothing more than a sequel
If there's any point, I want to stress
To change the state of leadership, we need to change the leadership selection and evaluation process
Will this ever happen is anyone's guess
Until then should we hope for more out of leaders but expect less?

About the Author

Vincent was born and raised in Virginia and works as an Audit Manager for the Federal Government. He received his bachelor's degree in accounting from Saint Paul's College and Master of Accounting and Financial Management from Keller School of Management. While in college Vincent participated in the ROTC program which sparked his passion for the art and science of leadership. Upon graduation Vincent was commissioned as an Officer in the United States Army to which he committed 21 years of honorable service. Vincent is also a leader and a pilar in his community serving as a head coach for a local youth track and field team. Vincent's dream is to educate and develop quality leaders using non-traditional forms of literature. When he's not reading or writing, Vincent enjoys working out and spending time with family and friends.

How to stay in touch with upcoming books from the author:

www.ingramcontent.com/pod-product-compliance
Lightning Source LLC
La Vergne TN
LVHW021230080526
838199LV00089B/5987